Living Flower Arrangements

Margaret Davis

LIVING
FLOWER
ARRANGEMENTS

ANGUS AND ROBERTSON

First published in 1971 by

ANGUS AND ROBERTSON (PUBLISHERS) PTY LTD
221 George Street, Sydney
54 Bartholomew Close, London
107 Elizabeth Street, Melbourne
89 Anson Road, Singapore

National Library of Australia Card Number & ISBN 0 207 12151 6

Printed in Hong Kong

Unless otherwise credited, all photography by Arthur Davis

Contents

TO MY MOTHER
to whom I shall always be indebted for the inheritance
of a love of gardens and flowers

Introduction

It has always seemed to me a little sad that a flower arrangement is so transient a thing. No matter how much care is taken in the preparation of cut flowers, they rarely last for more than a fraction of the lifetime of those left growing on the plant. Classic examples of this are those wonderful indoor growers, the cyclamens and the African violets. One can never cease to marvel at the length of time the flowers remain on these plants, yet cut them and put them in water, and their life ebbs away with the most depressing speed. Azaleas, too, although they will last a few days when cut, will remain fresh far longer when left on the plants, and even fuchsias, almost hopeless as cut flowers, will give pleasure for a considerable period if left growing undisturbed. In fact, it would be safe to say that most, if not all, flowers last longer when left growing, if — and this is a big "if" — they are not exposed to very strong sunlight and wind.

Here, of course, is where the potted flowering plants come into their own, especially those small enough and light enough to be brought into the house. I am very much in agreement with a writer who once said, "You get to *know* them better when you grow them in pots!" Not only do you get to know them, but you enjoy them so much more when they are right there beside you, in the middle of a busy life, to be seen and appreciated in all their stages from tight buds to fully opened flowers. A great deal of attention has been paid in recent years to the use of growing plants for interior decoration, and they are often essential to offset the severity of much of our modern architecture, both in homes and in public buildings. Picture windows and large areas of glass provide, in many cases, ideal conditions for the tropical and semi-tropical plants so widely used, but it seems as though the flowering plants have been much neglected in all these indoor garden schemes. Certainly it must be admitted that flowers need a little more care than the almost everlasting philodendrons, ficus, ivy, and similar evergreens now seen on all sides, but they are also infinitely more exciting and varied. Most of us would find our outdoor gardens much less interesting if they contained only foliage plants year in and year out, so why should we be content with this situation in our indoor gardens? Why even should we be content to have merely a few potted plants among the evergreens on the windowsill when they can play an infinitely more glamorous role as part of the decoration in so many places throughout the house?

Economically, there is an extremely stong argument in favor of using flowering plants in preference to cut flowers, for often a plant will cost no more than a dozen choice blooms. Not only will blooms left on the plant last much longer, but with reasonable care many plants will continue to grow on for years, if transferred into successively larger pots or to the garden. Moreover, apartment dwellers without gardens can always count on giving a lot of pleasure to garden-owning friends by handing on their plants when they grow too large for indoor life.

I remember once reading of how a large number of potted trees and shrubs were always included in the "paraphernalia of war" that accompanied Alexander the Great on his campaigns. They were set up round his tent when he camped, even if only briefly, whether to remind him of his homeland or as relief from the horrors of war, we shall never know. We certainly do know that all through the ages, right down to the present time, many outstanding men have turned to plants for relaxation and refreshment; the beautiful gardens created by Sir Winston Churchill are a classic example. We, too, in our much smaller spheres, can find peace and happiness beyond measure in the endless wonder of an opening flower.

How It All Began

One of the most interesting periods of my life was the time I spent studying both Bonsai and Japanese flower arrangement during my first visit to Japan. I had been lecturing, broadcasting, and writing on the subject of flower arrangement for some years prior to this journey and was most anxious to learn something about Ikebana, the art of Japanese flower arrangement, of which very little was known in the Western world at that time. It was the immediate postwar period, and all things Japanese were very much out of favor and out of fashion. The announcement that I even wished to go to Japan was received with incredulity and something like horror, so that when I finally took off for Tokyo it was with more than a little trepidation.

From my first day in Japan, however, it was obvious that my visit would be a happy and profitable one.

It was the height of spring, when all the great masters of Ikebana staged their best exhibitions, and I went from exhibition to exhibition and from lesson to lesson, notebook and camera always in hand, my brain reeling under the effort to remember and record all the beauty and ideas presented to it.

Every moment was fascinating, but perhaps most fascinating of all was the opportunity to compare and contrast the arts of Ikebana and Bonsai. On the one hand were the years of study to learn how to compose arrangements of flowers that, at best, could not be expected to last more than a few days; on the other, the emphasis on creating a growing plant designed to last perhaps for centuries.

Yet, despite this complete contrast in objectives, there were points of similarity of form, particularly in the arrangements of the Moribana style, where the flowers placed in the shallow containers were carefully arranged to give the appearance of growing, and in the taller arrangements, where stems were grouped together so that they appeared to be springing from a single main stem or root. Again and again, I encountered these efforts to create the effect of growth — iris grouped with leaves and buds as though growing, the painstaking reassembling of the little sheaths at the base of groups of narcissus, convolvulus trailing from baskets and hanging vases in a way that emulated its natural habits — and over and over the unworthy thought came to me that it would surely all be much easier, and the flowers would certainly last much longer, if they *were* actually growing!

These thoughts I kept strictly to myself, for the masters of both these art forms would, I felt sure, have regarded them as the veriest heresy. And so I continued to learn and to make copious notes, reflecting that obviously the artists who created these transient masterpieces of Ikebana were sufficiently rewarded in having created them, without being concerned that they would vanish forever in a few days, sometimes a few hours. All those delicately beautiful curving branches created by the painstaking insertion of tiny wedges, those fantastically complicated and difficult Rikka arrangements, those towering nine-foot structures that often dominated large exhibitions — and often not even a photograph would remain to pay tribute to the results of all this artistry and patience! I recall one day when, at an exhibition during the morning, I greatly admired a beautifully arranged branch of wisteria. In the afternoon, at my Bonsai class, I saw a growing wisteria so like the cut branch that it was impossible not to reflect on how much longer the beauty of the growing plant would last.

So, gradually, I turned more and more to growing plants in containers of all sorts, not all of Japanese influence — some, as you will see here, distinctly Western in form and derivation — but, whether Eastern or Western, all bringing to me the greatest joy and sense of achievement.

The author's living room.

4

Moss Gardens

One of the enthusiasms that I share with the people of Japan is a great love of moss in all its many forms. But it is not of the exquisite little Japanese gardens, nor of Kyoto's wonderful Saiho-ji Moss Garden that I am thinking at present, but of a moss garden designed to form the basis of a never-ending series of flower arrangements using cut flowers or growing plants, or a combination of both.

One of the many delightful things about moss is that, like many of the best things in life, it is absolutely free. You need not go to a nursery to buy moss; it comes to you. Given enough wet weather, damp rocks, or moist shaded places, sooner or later these lovely velvety green patches will appear. If they do not appear in your own garden, moss may easily be found in nearby damp places — roadside retaining walls, railway embankments, shaded woodland gullies. One Bonsai enthusiast I know, whose miniature trees are always set off by a beautiful carpet of moss, swears that suburban gutters are unequalled as a source of supply.

Having then found your moss, the next step is to lift it with as little disturbance as possible. I suggest that you take along the flat dish or tray in which it is to grow — this being first filled with soil, river sand, or peat moss — together with a pointing trowel, such as is used by bricklayers, rather than a curved garden trowel. With this tool you can lift a large section of the moss with a minimum of breakage, and it can then be pressed gently down on the soil in the dish. Water moss well, and always keep it moist, and, of

The cut-leaf maple *(Acer palmatum dissectum)* in this Moribana container has been lifted from a deeper pot to form this arrangement. The mound of soil is concealed by a grouping of stones and small pieces of driftwood that also serve to hold the saxatile tulips. The ground cover is helxine.

course, in a shaded place. Most of us have a shady corner somewhere in our territory, however small. If it will accommodate two or three trays of moss, of different sizes and shapes, then the enjoyment you will derive will be enormous. Each tray can hold a different variety of moss or perhaps an assortment of several kinds, for there are a great many mosses to be found if one takes the trouble to search for them. I have shown in the accompanying illustrations only a few of the many variations that can be played upon the theme of these basic moss gardens, and I feel sure that others will suggest themselves to you, using the flowers and plants available in your particular locality at different seasons.

Some of the ground-covering plants used in the arrangements illustrated are not really moss, although I have grouped them all under this heading. One such is *Helxine soleirolii,* also called "baby's tears" — and some very unflattering names by Bonsai growers who have introduced it as a ground cover in shallow containers with cherished Bonsai, only to find it eventually almost choking the larger plant with its close mat of roots and robust habit of growth. On shaded garden walls it is delightful, making a close green carpet either horizontally or vertically, and it is a simple matter to pull off just as much as is needed to cover the surface of any arrangement.

There are a number of suitable ground covers: Some of the prostrate thymes can be used in this way, and the beautiful gray-green lichens are unsurpassed if one can find them clinging to stones in damp areas. I have tried to keep these in my garden without any very great success, but if one is lucky enough to find small flat stones with lichens already growing on them, and can keep them in a damp place outdoors, they can be used over and over in many ways.

The branch of willow is growing under the moss. The hoop-petticoat daffodils have been added and are secured by spiked metal holders (known as needle holders), concealed in the moss. English daisies, violas, or other small flowers could be used here after the hoop-petticoat daffodils are spent. If the stems are thin, they can be held together with rubber bands before being impaled on the holders. A group of small holders can be useful in this case.

Combining Cut Flowers and Growing Plants

Not only can the little moss gardens play host to a seasonal assortment of growing plants, but they are invaluable as containers for a wide variety of combinations of growing plants and cut flowers. Some of these are shown here, but it will not require a great deal of imagination to visualize the endless succession of combinations that can be made throughout the year. The procedure is simple. One merely submerges a needle holder (a spiked metal base used in arranging flowers) in a hollow scooped out of the soil or sand beneath the moss. If the flowers are tall or very thirsty types, the holders that come encased in a small metal container can be used, and water kept in this. Alternatively, the holder can be placed inside a small round can about one inch deep. If only small or light flowers such as snowdrops, crocus, violets, or daisies are used, no holder will be needed; their stems will stand quite well in the soil or sand beneath the moss. Sand or very sandy soil is the best base for moss, because most flowers will last just as long in wet sand as in water. Obviously the sand must be kept wet for cut flowers. Sand has another advantage over water: it does not generate the unpleasant odor that sometimes comes when flower stems begin to decay in water.

The African violet and the ivy are growing with the moss in this container. The *Iris stylosa* are cut and held by a spiked base concealed in the moss. The same base holds the driftwood upright.

Driftwood makes a very good foil for many types of cut flowers and can be extremely decorative and interesting by itself or in combination with stones. Again the possibilities are endless, and the illustrations shown here will, I feel sure, spark off many other ideas for using the flowers and plants of your own area, wherever it may be.

Top. This little moss garden holds a permanent miniature papyrus. The willow branch will take root and grow on for a time. The polyanthus have been added from three-inch pots. These will continue to flower for several weeks if the arrangement is given good light and air. They can then be planted in the garden and their places filled by small later-flowering plants, perhaps violas or primulas. By this time the willow will be in leaf and will look very attractive for many weeks.

Bottom. The pussywillow in this container has taken root and will grow on until the catkins give way to leaves. A number of different cut flowers can be added during this time. Once the leaves have fully grown the pussywillow is best discarded or planted in the garden. The camellias used here are Hanafuki, sometimes known as Akebono, but all camellias blend beautifully with pussy-willow. Daffodils are also very effective in this type of arrangement.

Left. Winter scene. A Bonsai pine has been taken from its pot (it comes out very easily), its root ball surrounded by wet sand topped by moss (additional to that already growing under the pine), and the cut snowdrops have been pushed into the moss and sand. The whole is then covered by foam made by beating up some bath foam powder, which lasts for quite a few hours. Even after the "snow" has melted the arrangement will still be decorative for several days, or longer if the snowdrops are renewed. Do not keep Bonsai pines indoors for more than a week at a time: they need sun and air.

Right. Here is another container with its permanent moss planting, to which has been added a cut branch of *Magnolia soulangeana* supported by a needle holder and a piece of driftwood.

Left. The bamboo container has a permanent planting of moss in wet sand into which is sunk a needle holder to support the branch. A piece of driftwood adds to the effect and hides the holder.

Right. To the moss permanently growing in this container have been added the sprays of pussywillow and a flower of *Magnolia veitchii*, both supported on a long holder. The pussywillow will remain for several weeks, and even after its catkins fade the branches will be attractive with the young leaves that follow. By this time it will have taken root, and can be grown outdoors. When the magnolia fades it can be replaced by a succession of single flowers or groups of flowers.

The Useful Moribana Container

The Moribana type of container is extremely well suited to the low rectangular coffee tables now so widely used for interior decoration in both modern and period styles. These rectangular containers are popular in many schools of Japanese flower arrangement, flowers usually being arranged in them to represent a small landscape. There is typically a treelike branch at one end, a cluster of low-growing flowers at the other, and the holders supporting these are covered with moss or short juniper foliage to simulate growth.

The growing versions of this type of arrangement, several of which are shown here, have a similar effect, but these will last for years, as against a few days when cut flowers are used. The small base plants will need to be replaced as their flowers fade, but the maple and willow, which are the focal points, will only require occasional root-pruning and branch-trimming to keep them in the right proportions. The ground covers, being perennial, will continue to grow, also with occasional trimming and feeding.

A Macrantha azalea trained as a semi-cascade. The soft branches of young plants are easily adapted to this shape. The lower branch can be allowed to grow out horizontally for quite a distance as its wood hardens; but if a more symmetrical shape is preferred the shorter branch can be encouraged and the longer one nipped back. I love azaleas for their amenability to shaping into many different forms. Directions for growing a full cascade are given under "Azalea Margaret Davis".

Left. Spring. The crab apple shown here has been trained into a windblown shape. There are many varieties of crab apple, or pyrus, and small grafted types make beautiful Bonsai. Cydonia *(Chaenomeles)* is very suitable also for this type of arrangement. The ground cover here is helxine. It grows freely out of doors in temperate climates, and is easily lifted in large sections from rocks or pathways. Transferred to a shallow container, it will continue to grow happily on either sand, soil, or peat moss. The polyanthus were bought in tiny plastic pots, and knocked out to be bedded in the soil of the container.

Right. Summer. Summer calls for color, and we find it here in the glowing red of *Billbergia pyramidalis,* its color repeated by the capsicums, with grapes and a custard apple for contrast. The billbergia, which has a surprisingly small root system, is in a pot concealed by some flat driftwood. It will remain healthy indoors for quite long periods, and the fruit in the container can be changed and varied.

Left. Autumn. Here the story is told by the vivid color of a branch of rhus, impaled on a needle holder concealed by the tall stone. The African violet was lifted from its shallow pot and planted in the soil of the container topped by moss and helxine.

Right. Winter. This moss garden has been covered with foam bath "snow", and a snow-covered branch of magnolia added to give height. The branch is impaled on a needle holder hidden in the moss, and the hellebore (Christmas Rose) shares the same holder. The small groups of snowdrops are kept firm by having rubber bands around the base of their stems, and they are then inserted into the soil in which the moss is growing. It is easiest to make a hole with a pencil to take the stems. Press the soil firmly around them if necessary. They will last just as long here as in water, but the soil must be kept quite moist. As the season progresses their place can be taken by other small flowers.

Like the moss gardens, these arrangements can be varied endlessly with the seasons, for even when maple and willow are bare their forms will still be decorative, and well suited to the wintry scenes that can be created by adding foam "snow" and base plantings of snowdrops or hellebore.

Moribana containers can be bought either with or without drainage holes, the former being for Bonsai, the latter for flower arrangements. Either can be used for growing arrangements, depending upon the plantings used. For a maple, a Bonsai container with a hole should be chosen, since maples must have a well-drained soil; if a willow is the main feature, the container without a hole is better, and wisteria can also be used, for both these plants are happy with wet feet. Moss, too, will be quite at home in these conditions. The container without a hole has the further advantage of not needing to be stood on a tray to catch the water.

All such plantings will benefit from periods out of doors in sun and fresh air to strengthen their growth, though care must be taken since some plants can easily have too much sun. Maples, for example, prefer semi-shade. Give frequent overhead sprinklings to remove house dust during these outdoor periods and spray with liquid soluble fertilizer. When crab

Top. The "snow" that covers the moss is made by whipping up a small amount of bath foam. It will last throughout an evening, and has very much the effect of melting snow as it gradually evaporates and the moss reappears. The snowdrops are not growing. They have been cut and inserted in groups in the soil beneath the moss. The bare branches of the corkscrew willow, which is growing in the container, have been dusted with flour to simulate snow.

Bottom. *Wisteria multijuga alba* (or *floribunda alba*) is pale pink in the bud and when the flowers first open, but it then fades to white. This plant is now about twelve years old: I had to wait eight years before it began to flower. This sometimes happens with the more unusual types of wisteria, but they are worth waiting for when they finally produce a plant like this. I prune the roots of this one once a year, after flowering, cutting back the branches at the same time. Long growths are cut back during the year.

apples, prunus, or similar fruiting plants are used, it is best after they have flowered to leave them out of doors until the next flowering season to allow them to form their fruit and to have enough sun to form the next season's flowers. All these plants require as much sun as you can give them. If you have not enough large oblong bowls to set out, it is a simple matter to lift any of the plants for their period out of doors and place them in smaller but still shallow Bonsai pots. This also applies to wisteria when it is out of season, for, like the flowering trees, it is not particularly attractive when not in flower and is best relegated to the background.

If space is too limited to accommodate more than one of the very large Moribana containers, the same one can be used all the year indoors. Its contents can be varied with the seasons by growing a series of different plants in the same plain shallow Bonsai pots, transferring them to the large Moribana container when at their peak. The plants may be returned to the smaller Bonsai pots when flowering is finished. Azaleas are ideal for this purpose, with their wide range of shapes and compact root systems. By using a succession of types that flower at different times, azaleas can be featured for many months. The little Gumpos can be used for the low plantings and the taller Kurumes or Indicas for the "tree" end of the arrangement.

If you wish to use a plant from a pot which may be a little deeper than the moss or ground cover in the container, the extra height of soil is easily concealed by covering it with a further layer of the ground cover plant or with a few curved stones or sections of flattish driftwood. This mound effect will, if anything, look better than an entirely flat surface.

Some people become extremely nervous at the thought of removing plants from their pots; they need not be over-concerned. Many of the plants used in these arrangements will have been grown as Bonsai, in order to obtain the mature treelike forms, and will therefore require removal from their pots at yearly, and sometimes half-yearly, intervals to have their roots pruned and the soil replaced. (See "Flowering Bonsai.") Even when annuals are used for ground planting, these will usually be sufficiently root-bound in the small pots to suffer no harm in being transferred to your large oblong container.

Azalea Arrangements

I always feel quite depressed at the sight of an azalea in full bloom being drenched by heavy rain, and if the rain is accompanied by wind, it is even more depressing to know that all that beauty, all those lovely delicate flowers, will so soon be a thing of the past. This is why I prefer to grow azaleas in containers, and it is also why the Davis household gets very crowded indeed during periods of prolonged wet weather. Pots of azaleas stand on tables, windowsills, on the floor, and of course in every available spot on the veranda, which is really our main living area. It was after one unusually prolonged wet spell that we decided to enlarge this useful veranda so that there would be more room for all of us, and both Davises and azaleas have greatly benefited from this decision. How wise, I often think, were the Victorians and Edwardians to build conservatories where delicate plants such as these could be sheltered and enjoyed at close quarters! Alas, those spacious conservatories would be prohibitively costly for most budgets in our day. Still, even the smallest household should be able to find room for at least a few growing flowers. While we may not have conservatories, most modern homes do have large window areas, which were certainly not a feature of Victorian houses, and these provide the ideal condition of light needed for both indoor plants and those brought in for limited periods, such as azaleas.

Just how limited this period will be is largely determined by the variety of azalea and by the conditions in the room in which it is to be kept. Not only the amount of light and air but the method of heating must be considered. For instance, gas-fire heating is anathema to most plants, so if this is your only means of heating try to put your plants in a protected place out of doors during periods when the room is likely to be closed up.

Try also to provide a position where plants can get a good deal of fresh air without being placed in strong draughts.

Watering is important to azaleas, and their soil should not be allowed to dry out at any time. But do not overdo the watering to the extent of leaving the pots standing in saucers of water for long periods. The question of just when to water is impossible to answer without knowing the conditions; climate, room temperature, heating, all play a part in a decision that only you can make. I find that by feeling the soil surface I can judge whether it is still sufficiently damp. If space permits, it is a good idea to take all plants outside once a week and sprinkle the soil surface with a fine hose sprinkler or a can, wetting the flowers as little as possible. If you have no suitable place to do this, let them stand in the kitchen sink, soaking up as much water as possible for ten minutes or so.

I shall not attempt to enumerate the many varieties of azaleas, for their numbers increase almost daily, and many of the new hybrids seem very well suited to living indoors for long periods. One such hybrid is Sweetheart Supreme, illustrated here, which, in addition to its long flowering period, has a very attractive spreading habit if allowed to grow horizontally, though it also responds well to training in upright forms. There are many similar hybrids in this category, and it is well worth experimenting with as many as you can find space for.

All the azaleas in this group are of the late-flowering Macrantha type. It is surprising that these azaleas are not more widely grown, although the Gumpos, the smaller members of the family, are being seen more frequently. Their flowering takes place in very late spring or even early summer, after the Indica varieties have long ceased blooming, and they therefore need some protection from the heat of the sun when in flower. This makes them very suitable for keeping indoors. Also, their flowers hold well, and the branches are generally amenable to shaping. Those with softer more spreading habit adapt well to training as cascades (one of these can be seen at the top of the stand). I did not use wire in training this one. Azalea branches are extremely brittle and break easily, and the very soft branches of this plant allowed it to weep downwards. All that was needed was some elimination of the higher branches to divert strength to the lower ones.

Left. Azalea Deutsche Perle is quite an old variety, but still one of the best. It holds its flowers extremely well, especially if the plants are brought indoors just as the buds begin to unfold. In this way it is protected from rain and wind, and the flowers will last for many weeks indoors if given an airy, light room. This is quite a young plant, but already beginning to assume the graceful form that is characteristic of the variety.

Right. A Macrantha azalea as a semi-cascade. First the branches are anchored with wire to the side of the pot to keep them horizontal, then some of the side branches are allowed to grow out, the others being kept shorter and their tips being nipped until the required shape is formed. For details see the section on Azalea Margaret Davis.

Left. Azalea Dr Bergman is a lovely salmon pink Belgian double, very suitable to container culture and to growing in Bonsai form. It is an easy one to shape, and has a fairly long flowering period, lasting very well indoors. When grown in this way, it needs to have pulled off the many small shoots this variety tends to put out from the base of the plant. These can be used for cuttings.

Right. Azalea Iceberg is a fast-growing double. Although it may not hold its flowers as long as Deutsche Perle it is well worth growing, and is a good variety for shaping. The scroll in the background was painted in Hong Kong by Chow Chien Chiu.

Perhaps the azaleas most widely used for growing in pots are what are generally known as the "Belgian Doubles," though some of them aren't really doubles at all. They have been grown in Belgian and Dutch nurseries for many years especially for the florist trade, and they appear as most welcome patches of color in European shops throughout the early spring. They are also widely grown in Australia and in the United States. Although some of these grow well in the open garden, most appear to be happiest growing in pots.

Quite often a certain amount of shaping can be done during the flowering period. Removing each dead flower as soon as possible will not only prolong the flowering period but will stimulate new shoots below the old flower, especially if a little of the stem also is removed.

Soil for azaleas must never contain lime. A mixture containing about one-third peat moss, one-third sandy soil, and one-third leaf mould is quite good, or you can buy ready-packaged azalea and camellia soils.

Top. Kurume azalea Azuma Kagami is one of my favorites. Its delicately lovely pink flowers bloom in splendid profusion; it can flourish indoors for incredibly long periods when in flower; and it is most amenable to shaping and training. Whether a tall plant or a gracefully spreading one is required, this lovely little azalea will fill the bill. One has only to prune, after flowering: the lower shoots if tall growth is wanted, and the top growth if a spreading plant is preferred. Everybody should have at least one Azuma Kagami.

Bottom. Sweetheart Supreme was raised in the United States only a few years ago. It is not surprising that it has become enormously popular. Like Azuma Kagami, it is ideally suited to indoor decoration, and is similarly amenable to training, having a particularly attractive spreading habit if the lower branches are encouraged, and the upper ones shortened back. It makes beautiful "up-and-down" Ikebana-type arrangements also.

Azalea Margaret Davis

I imagine it is natural to be a little biased toward a plant that bears one's name, but by any other name this would still be my favorite azalea, if only for its graceful and very adaptable habit of growth. Add to this an extreme hardiness, a remarkable freedom from pests and diseases, and you have an azalea that is outstanding by any standards.

Like most of the Macrantha azaleas from which this seedling came, it lends itself perfectly to growing as a Bonsai, for its sturdy, quickly growing stems soon take on an aged appearance, and the gracefully arching branches contribute to the usual treelike form. Most of those illustrated here are relatively young plants, raised from cuttings.

This azalea will take a good deal of sun, though it should be brought into a shaded position when the flowers are ready to open. If taken indoors at this stage, the flowers will last very well, provided the plant is kept moist and in a room that is well ventilated but free from strong draughts.

After flowering, trim the plants to the shape desired and remove any weak, spindly growths. If a treelike form is desired, break off the strong

This picture gives an idea of the form of Azalea Margaret Davis when it is allowed to grow naturally, without being trained to any particular shape. It is pruned, however, just after flowering to induce additional flower buds for next season. This is the time to feed azaleas, usually with a light topping of old cow manure (or other suitable lime-free mulch). It is not necessary to give artificial fertilizer, but if animal manure is unprocurable, applications of soluble fertilizer can be given every few weeks for three or four months after flowering.

shoots that tend to form from the base of the plant; these will make very good cuttings if placed in a pot of damp sand and kept in a shaded place. (Always put cuttings round the edges of the pots. They seem to root better in this way, especially in terracotta pots.)

If you wish to restrict the growth of your plants, a good time to prune the roots is while shaping and pruning the branches. As this plant has a strong root system, one third of the roots can be cut away, the old soil shaken or hosed off, and the plant repotted into either ready-prepared azalea or camellia mixture or a mixture of one third each of peat moss, sandy soil, and leaf mould, with a light topping of lime-free mulch.

It can be rewarding to plant the seeds that form very freely on this and other Macranthas, for, like camellias, azaleas do not always come true to the parent, and very interesting new types sometimes result with differences in both form and color. This azalea, for instance, is similar in color, but not in habit, to the wild mauve azaleas seen in parts of Japan, whence its parents originally came. There, they grow enormously tall. I saw some beautiful specimens in the lovely Saiho-ji Moss Garden, towering among the Japanese maples round the lake, their delicate mauve flowers beautifully contrasting with the pale golden-green of the freshly opening maple leaves.

Azalea Margaret Davis growing as a cascade. One often finds an azalea with a low-swooping branch, and this makes a good starting point. Shorten back the other branches, and let the low one grow horizontally for a time. In Japan branches are wired to shape them, but this can be risky, for azalea branches break very easily. I find it simpler to tie a wire around the pot and simply hook the main azalea branch to this. Do not force it too suddenly. The wire can be gradually shortened.

The best time for additional training is immediately after flowering, when all growths not conforming to the desired shape can be cut back, and those on the cascading branches shortened just enough to stimulate additional growth where it is wanted. This is also the time for feeding and, if necessary, for either root-pruning or potting in a larger-sized container.

The Dainty Gumpos

The delightful dwarf azaleas known as the "Gumpos" have only recently been widely grown outside Japan, though they have long been used for Bonsai in that country. They are also called "Satsuki," though this name is also given to taller-growing forms of the same variety. The group to which these little ones belong is also known in some regions as Macrantha azaleas. (The naming of azaleas is a very complicated subject, which needs a book to itself.) For some reason these Macrantha or Satsuki types are not always easy to come by, but it is worth searching about for them, for they are very hardy and very adaptable, growing equally well in temperate and cold climates. They flower later than most other varieties, which I find an advantage because it is delightful to have them come just when all the glorious spring flush of the main varieties is over.

This collection of Gumpo azaleas gives an idea of the range of colors of these attractive little dwarfs. Members of the late-flowering Macrantha family of azaleas, they like the same conditions as those given in the directions for Azalea Margaret Davis, and I have found, in fact, that they seem to need quite an amount of winter sun to make satisfactory flower buds. The Gumpos have a fairly strong root system, and therefore need a reasonable amount of feeding, especially if kept in small containers. Do not keep them in the sun while they are in flower. The sun will shorten the life of the flowers, which will otherwise last very well indoors on protected windowsills.

The little Gumpos do not remain in flower as long as some varieties, but they are so decorative that it is well worth buying them if only to enjoy them for a few weeks. When flowering is finished, give them a fairly sunny place out of doors; they will take more sun than most other azaleas. All azaleas benefit from a light topping of old cow manure or a suitable fertilizer after flowering is finished, and this is also the time for pruning and shaping. Cut off all dead and twiggy growths. If you are planning a special shape, work toward it, either by tying the branches down lightly with copper wire for a pendulous effect or by removing surplus base growths from the main stem if you aim at a Bonsai effect. Prunings can then be used for cuttings, and they will root quite readily in a pot of damp sand kept in a shaded place.

Flowers That Bloom in the Night

There is something tremendously fascinating about flowers that open only when night falls. Of all the wonderful tropical flowers that abound in Thailand, those I remember most vividly are the waterlilies that opened around us as darkness fell when we visited the exquisite pavilion of Princess Chumbhot's palace in Bangkok. Built out over a small lake, and filled with treasures of Thai art, the pavilion is shaded by tropical trees and vines, a cool retreat from Bangkok's oppressive heat. Here the princess serves wonderful Thai food to a never-ending stream of visitors from all over the world. Art lovers, garden lovers, kings, presidents — all come to revel in the beauty created by this most charming and talented lady.

Another cherished memory is of a hot night in Hong Kong, the first night of our stay at the old Repulse Bay Hotel. As we dined on the veranda, the manager brought to our table a handful of moonflowers just uncurling their beautifully pleated buds. To watch the opening of a flower is, to me, a never-failing excitement, and the moonflower opens so quickly — one minute a little white furled umbrella, the next a slight quivering, a half-opened umbrella, and then a wonderful round white flower! And with the final movement comes a rush of perfume.

After dinner we were taken to a courtyard at the rear of the hotel, where the enormous vine was literally covered with these snow-white disks of bloom. Immediately my covetous gardener's eye lit upon some well-filled seed-pods among the flowers. Could I have one, please? And so, only a year later, we were able to watch on our own veranda this miracle of the opening of moonflowers. And because I can never resist growing things in pots, it was not long before they were opening right in the living room, and here you see one of these. So easy to grow, for they belong to the robust convolvulus family, and they ask only for a reasonably good soil and as much warmth as possible. Full sun is desirable, and the plants in pots must be taken back into the sun next morning after being enjoyed indoors or they become leggy and drawn. I have seen a pink form of moonflower listed in catalogues, and I mean to get it some day. It could not be as wonderful as this glorious white one, I feel sure, but I would still love to see it.

Yet another tropical night in another year saw us in Honolulu, dining in one of the wonderful gardens with which Hawaii abounds. Again tightly furled white flowers were growing beside the veranda (though in Hawaii, it's a lanai, of course). This time it was a completely different flower, the night-blooming cereus, one of the cactus family. Again we experienced the wave of perfume, much stronger than that of the moonflower, and increasing in intensity as the night wears on, so much so that it could be difficult to sleep close to these flowers.

I obtained no seeds this time, so the flower remained just a beautiful memory until one day I saw it, or a very closely related member of its family, growing in lush profusion in the lovely garden of our good friend Norman Wallis, who had brought it years ago from Burma. It was not long, of course, before a cutting was growing in our garden, but like so many cuttings that find their way into this garden, confined to a pot so that later it could be enjoyed at close quarters. On summer nights there can be the unromantic note of buzzing mosquitoes to spoil watching the miracle of the opening of these flowers, so we all go indoors where the white petals are enhanced by the background of blue curtains and carpets. Not much

The moonflower, a night-flowering white convolvulus. Although it is a fast and robust climber, the moonflower can be easily grown in a small pot, provided that it is well fertilized, either with animal manure or a general fertilizer, either in tablet or soluble form. The fast-growing stems need support in the form of driftwood or branches.

work is done on these nights, when we keep going back to marvel at the wonderful mass of stamens, at the petals opening wider and wider as the night wears on, knowing that by breakfast time they will be a limp, soggy mass.

Like the moonflowers, the cereus are quick-growing plants, of which there are many varieties, all beautiful. They need a rich soil, plenty of sun and warmth, and a reasonable amount of moisture. They should be repotted every two years or so.

Queen of the Night cactus or Malaysian Lily *(Selenicereus nocturnus)*. This is the lovely night-blooming cereus described in the accompanying chapter. There are a number of varieties and it is found in many countries, usually tropical or semi-tropical, but it is easily grown in a heated greenhouse, or without heat if the climate is not too cold. It will grow into a very large plant in the ground, being naturally a strong climber. The flowers are beautifully perfumed, but last only for one night.

The plant illustrated was grown from a leaf cutting, and is only one and a half years old. It needs a rich soil, and plenty of water.

The Gay Cyclamen

The cyclamen, which provides splashes of color in living rooms in many different countries, surely deserves better of us than the usual presentation of a single plant in a dreary earthenware or plastic pot standing in an equally dreary saucer!

A whole row of cyclamen can decorate a room throughout the winter if they are given a windowsill that catches an hour or so of morning sun. There are many such windowsills in these days of large picture windows, but if a large glass area is not available, why not try a group of three or four plants in a wrought-iron stand as close as possible to the glass of a smaller window? Light is essential for healthy growth, and some morning sun is also necessary, but given these conditions, plus regular watering, the cyclamen will produce an incredible number of blooms and continuing crops of new buds for a very long time.

Top. This row of cyclamen on my dining-room windowsill gets about an hour's morning sun, which suits them very well, for they continue to flower there for four or five months every winter. The wire pot-holders are convenient containers into which to place the pots. They have a built-in saucer at the base of each. See text for growing directions.

Bottom. The old-fashioned wire stand is useful for displaying cyclamen, and it allows each plant to have the good light it needs. The stand can be moved to various parts of the house or patio, to discover which position best suits these lovely flowers.

The method of watering is extremely important in the maintenance of healthy plants. It is imperative that the water be poured just inside the rim of the pots and not into the center of the plants. The latter method accounts for a great many casualties, since it can cause rotting of the new buds and leaves and eventually of the bulbs. There are many types of thin-spouted cans available these days, and these are ideal, not only for getting under the leaves at the edges of the pots, but for filling flower vases. Failing such a can, a thin-spouted teapot will serve the purpose.

It is difficult to give exact directions as to when and how often to water. A good rule is to test the soil by feeling it with your finger. If it is quite wet, do not water; aim at keeping the surface slightly damp. Some people prefer to let water be absorbed from the base of the pot by filling the saucer in which it is standing, but it is unwise to allow water to remain in the saucer for long periods. Pots standing in deep containers should be lifted out after three or four days to make sure they are not standing in too much water.

I always give my plants a thorough overhead sprinkling once a week, taking them outdoors on a day when there is no wind and gently spraying all over both flowers and leaves with the finest sprinkling jet of the hose. If conditions make a hose impracticable, use an atomizer. I do this sprinkling in the evening and then leave the plants outside all night, making sure they are in a sheltered place, protected from wind. Even in quite cold weather this exposure to the night air seems to benefit them greatly, and plants that have begun to look a little limp and tired from remaining too long indoors will stiffen up amazingly. Take care, however, that when they are brought indoors the sun is not allowed to shine on leaves and flowers that are still wet. It is best to gently shake off surplus water and let the plants dry off in shade, otherwise you may find burnt patches on the delicate flowers.

A two-year-old cyclamen, its pot placed in a Wedgwood jardiniere.

44

Every second week I add some soluble fertilizer to the water during this spraying process. There are many types of good liquid fertilizer to be bought, usually containing urea, which is excellent for maintaining healthy growth throughout the flowering season. I do not find it necessary to give any additional fertilizer.

Perhaps I should sound a warning about the method of removing spent flowers and leaves, having in the past damaged some good plants by jerking them out by the stems. To my dismay, I once found a clump of five or six buds and some leaves adhering to the stem I had pulled out! Now I twist the stems carefully, holding them near their base. They can be cut low down, of course, but the remaining stem section will later have to be removed because it will begin to rot.

I am constantly asked whether the plants can be carried on from year to year, and this can certainly be done, but it is very seldom indeed that a plant which has bloomed well for three or four months will be satisfactory the next year, and so I find it better to discard them altogether when flowering is finished and start with fresh plants the next season.

Top. The gaiety of the various colors of cyclamen can brighten a room for many months during the longest winter. The cyclamen is almost a universal indoor plant, being adaptable to either cold or reasonably warm climates. If the climate is warm, let the plants have a night out of doors occasionally on a sheltered patio or balcony. This will put new vitality into leaves and flowers inclined to droop if left too long in heated rooms. A fine spray over the tops of the plants will also help.

Bottom. Three pots of cyclamen are here held in a wide Japanese bamboo basket, lined with heavy foil to hold the water overflowing from the pots when they are watered.

Ways with African Violets

It is not surprising that the African violet (*Saintpaulia*) is often described as "America's favorite house plant," and it would surely qualify for this title in many countries. It would be difficult indeed to find another plant so ideally suited to growing indoors, difficult also to find one that continues to flower for such long periods once it finds a position to its liking. But, to quote Hamlet, "Ay, there's the rub!"—to find the position to its liking. This can be an extremely tantalizing and frustrating exercise, and one sometimes quite beyond the powers of even the most experienced and knowledgeable of gardeners, even when they are endowed with houses containing a wide variety of windows, one of which might reasonably be expected to suit these charming but, let's face it, capricious little plants.

On the other hand, I have known people with no knowledge whatever of

Dining-table arrangement combining African violets with grapes. These grapes are real, but it is possible to buy very convincing artificial ones, to be used when grapes are out of season.

The violet at the top has been taken gently out of its pot and placed in a cup-shaped flower-holder. This was designed by Constance Spry to fit into a candle-stick, so that flowers could surround the candles. The little funnel that goes into the candlestick will take care of surplus water so that the plant is not in danger of having wet feet. The plants on the mirror base are in shallow white plastic pots, masked by finely chopped cellophane left from some Christmas packing. This shredded cellophane has many uses, and gives a light, festive air to table decorations. This decoration will last for quite a long time if the light in the room is good.

48

even the first principles of gardening who grow African violets to perfection. These fortunate ones just happen to have a window, usually a kitchen window, that has the right aspect, the right amount of warmth and humidity, and the right amount of light. "What do you do to them?" query the envious ones, confronted with plants laden with blooms month in and month out. "Don't do a thing," is usually the reply. "Just water them occasionally." And this is how it goes. Position is all important. Like that indefinable charm, either you have it or you do not. Depressing, isn't it? I should know, for I am one of those experienced and reasonably knowledgeable characters described above, even one with a variety of windows, yet my African violets are mediocre at best. My kitchen, alas, has its windows shaded by too many trees, and none of the other windows seems to quite meet the requirements.

Yet all is not lost for those of us in this plight; there is still a ray of hope —or, I should say, a ray of light. Quite literally a ray of light—neon or fluorescent light, or better still, a special "Gro-lux" light, any of which can be installed in a window or built into a special tray so that it can be moved to different parts of the house. Any enterprising carpenter or electrician can do this, making something to fit the available places. I had one made to fit a twenty-inch tube, which was mounted above a shallow metal tray. A strip of metal at each end supports the light tube with a small metal canopy above it, and the whole thing is painted white to match the woodwork of the windowsill, on which it just fits. In the bathroom we built one into the woodwork at the top of the window, but because this light proved to be too far above the plants on the sill, I had a shelf put in half way up, with another light tube screwed underneath it, so that we now have two tiers of African violets, each well lighted, and looking very attractive when they are in bloom.

African violets blend well with gloxinias, which is not surprising, since they are members of the same family. The vivid color of this red gloxinia provides a good foil for the softer shades of the violets.

Opinions differ as to the best strength for these lights; some growers use two forty-watt tubes suspended eight inches above the plants, others prefer them a little higher, others say that an eighty-watt light placed fifteen inches above the plants is best. Again, results vary according to the variety of the violets, some of which take more light than others. If the plants acquire a bleached or scorched look, it is obvious that the light is too strong for them. Only by experimenting in your own particular environment can the perfect arrangement be found.

The lights must not be left on over the plants day and night. Twelve hours each day is sufficient, though some commercial growers force plants along by keeping them under lights for fifteen to sixteen hours a day. I have several friends who have the right conditions to grow these lovely flowers to perfection. One of them has a huge, bright sunroom where, in addition to pots on tables, windowsills, and stands holding violets of every conceivable color, there is a large white-painted traymobile-like structure fitted with a heating element for winter use. Here, on the white gravel-covered shelves is a wonderful array of flowers throughout the year.

Top. The pink African violet *(Saintpaulia)* growing in the white Chinese pot has cut branches of pussywillow inserted into the soil at the edges of the pot. Pussywillow is easily coaxed into these curving forms by bending each branch, holding it between two thumbs and directing it by the forefingers. Bend gently, taking care not to dislodge the catkins. The branches will remain in the curves. Do not leave the pussywillow too long, for it has a strong root system and will quickly outgrow the pot. It will be a few weeks before this happens, but by that time the catkins will have begun to fade and the branches can be gently removed from the soil — with a hand held over the violets' roots so that they will not be unduly disturbed.

Bottom. Table arrangement of a group of African violets, grown and arranged by Mrs Robert Oliver. She has placed two plants growing in shallow white plastic pots in an attractive soapstone bowl.

The plants are in a mixture of equal parts of sand, old lime-free manure, and leaf mould, and they are watered with warm water only when the surface soil looks and feels slightly dry.

As with other plants we have discussed, it is impossible to make hard and fast rules on the subject of watering. The season, humidity, room temperature, and heating must all be taken into consideration, but overwatering is often the reason for failure. Plants in containers must be watched to see that they are not left standing for long periods in surplus water. A layer of gravel or shell-grit in the bottom of the containers or in the saucer underneath the pots will keep them sufficiently raised. The water underneath the gravel will provide valuable humidity without reaching the base of the pots. African violets like humid conditions, and this is why they are so happy in the steamy atmosphere of a kitchen, or even in a well-lit bathroom. One grower I know who gets good results puts several cups of boiling water among her plants from time to time, and maintains that the resultant steam helps them along.

Another hint worth trying, this time from a California friend who is never without flowers, is to water the plants occasionally with weak tea. Apparently the acidity of the tea is beneficial. Some growers pin their faith on monthly applications of liquid soluble fertilizer, of which there are several good brands on the market, including the malodorous but very effective fish emulsion. In all cases, strengths given in the directions for these fertilizers must be halved for all potted plants, and it must also be remembered that fertilizer should never be applied when the soil is dry. Do not fertilize during winter.

African violets again. East meets West in this arrangement, with the traditional Italian alabaster bird bowl, and Quan Yin, Chinese Goddess of Mercy.

Wonderful Stones

Small or large, sandstone or ironstone, waterworn or volcanic, moss-covered or shiny — stones are wonderful. The Japanese have exhibitions of stones, connoisseurs' pieces, some black or gray, with perfect white chrysanthemums ingrained into them, costing thousands of yen; others like miniature mountains with waterfalls coursing down their slopes; others every shade of red or blue, or white as snow, or jet black; and each one mounted on its own perfectly carved wooden stand, or in a shallow tray of white pebbles.

Though we cannot all collect these Japanese treasures, there are many beautiful stones to be had, just for the picking up. Do not, of course, do your picking up in the National Parks or you may yourself be picked up by an alert ranger!

I admit there are plenty of stones that are just stones, just as there are lots of people who are just people, with no obvious personality to set them apart; but take one of these plain old stones and set it in a very damp place and give it a little moss to start it off, or even cover it with moss if you cannot wait for it to grow its own, and see if in a few weeks it isn't a thing of beauty. There is an affinity in moss and stones that is the perfect marriage. And with moss, of course, I also think of the wonderful grey-green lichen. Any ordinary stone coated or even streaked with this beautiful material cannot fail to be transformed. A little shaping might be helpful first: a too-square stone might benefit from having its corners knocked off, or a too-round one might have a few hollows cut into it. One need not be a sculptor to do this simple thing. If you are lucky enough to live in a district where there are volcanic stones, or seaside or river-worn stones that are already full of hollows, then try using these hollows to grow tiny trees or African violets or any small plants. They can be laid on the surface of the moss gardens, or just on shallow trays by themselves. (One can sometimes find such stones in shops that sell aquarium equipment.) These holey stones are enormously useful, too, for holding a piece of driftwood firmly in place. If the wood does not fit firmly enough, it can often be secured with a little modelling or florist's clay, or plasticine.

Stones of this type are much in demand by Bonsai enthusiasts for the miniature tray gardens now becoming popular in both East and West. The taller ones are planted with tiny cascading pines, azaleas or maples; the more squat ones may hold more spreading plants, and possibly form little water pools.

Sometimes the stones are placed in shallow trays of water. In other cases they rest upon a bed of tiny white pebbles. But a bed of moss is the most popular setting for stones, for its bright green gives life and interest at all times of the year. Chunky pieces of white marble can be beautiful placed on a bed of moss, to be used either as decoration in themselves, or as support for some cut flowers: orchids, magnolias, gardenias or camellias.

Life can never be dull once the eye has become trained to look for beautiful stones, for age certainly cannot wither, nor custom stale, their infinite variety.

Variations on a Driftwood Theme

So popular has driftwood become for flower arrangement and for combining with growing plants that good pieces can now be bought in many stores and nurseries. This is certainly a much quicker process than searching seashores, riverbeds, and high mountains, though many people enjoy the search and take a special pleasure in the pieces they have found for themselves. The main problem these days is that of storage for large pieces. If your home is small, however, even one piece can be used in a great variety of ways, only some of which are shown here.

White Czar camellia growing in a white Chinese glazed container. This is quite a young plant, having been bought in a four-inch pot. It is a good variety that holds its flowers well; but, since most single white camellias tend to drop their flower-heads before they are spent, I usually pin the heads on, driving a fine pin through the calyx. This forestalls the depressing plop of falling heads, so often heard by the hostess just as the guests are due to arrive. If the falling heads beat you to it, a little cheating is excusable. Pin other heads on, or insert a cut branch from a garden plant into the soil to help out (always supposing you have the same or a similar variety growing outside). The ideal way, of course, is to take cuttings of favorite garden plants for use indoors in this way (most types will flower in a couple of years): then the parent plant can be drawn upon for reinforcement on special occasions.

The piece of driftwood gives interest and height. It has a narrow point that fits easily into the soil at the back of the pot. If you do not have such a piece, a shorter one can be adapted by binding it with a piece of strong wire. This can then be inserted into the soil, supported, if necessary, with a small stone.

This S-shaped piece has been one of my treasures for nearly twenty years, ever since I first began to take an interest in flower arrangement. In those early days it was quite a novelty. When I tired of using it with cut flowers it acted as a support for my first philodendron; in time the philodendron outgrew it, and the piece was relegated to the cellar for a few years. Now it has been unearthed and dusted and scrubbed once more to serve with both cut flowers and growing plants.

Its original base had rotted badly from long immersion in water and soil, so a strong flat-bottomed piece of wood was found to hold it upright, and the driftwood can now be used alone, or in some of the ways shown here. I have not glued it permanently to the new base; it can be held firmly enough with a little modelling clay, so that it can be detached to support flowers in one of the moss-garden settings.

If you have tall pieces of driftwood you will find that their usefulness can be doubled if a suitable base can be found. Lighter pieces, such as are used in tall vases with flowers, can be attached to a strong needle holder with perhaps a little clay to help hold them if the base of the wood is not too hard. Stones can be used effectively, both to support driftwood and to add to the decorative effect of the shallow-bowl arrangements.

This is *Billbergia pyramidalis,* a very showy and easily grown bromeliad. Here it is in a four-inch pot, in a very open soil mixture, with one-third gravel in the bottom for drainage. These plants have very small roots and will therefore remain in small containers for long periods, needing little nourishment, provided that the vase-shaped leaf clusters are kept filled with water. They do not require full sun; the light should be good.

Top. The African violet in this picture has been given a piece of driftwood to add weight to the arrangement. The driftwood has a narrow pointed base: it has been sharpened at the base for use in this way, so that it can be driven into the pots without disturbing the plants growing in them. There is enough depth in the glazed pot to hold it upright.

Bottom. The driftwood serves as a dramatic background to the Gumpo azalea, the container of which is concealed by the base of the wood. The little Neapolitan cyclamen at the left are growing in the bowl of moss.

The S-curved driftwood is used here to give height to a moss garden arrangement in a Moribana container. The "moss" is helxine. It is a very attractive ground cover, and can be lifted easily in layers from the garden or from the stones over which it likes to grow, and laid on a bed of either soil or peat moss, where it will continue to grow for long periods if kept reasonably damp and in a good light.

The African violet is also growing in this container, and cut flowers such as the group of *Iris stylosa* can be added from time to time to give more color and interest. A small spiked holder (needle holder) keeps the flowers erect and is hidden under the helxine. If necessary, a rubber band can be used to hold the flower stems together.

If you have an early Victorian glass dome in the attic, you are indeed fortunate. If you have not, it is worth while searching about in the antique shops for one, for there are so many ways in which it can be used to feature indoor arrangements, and it can become a wonderful miniature conservatory to shelter a great variety of plants.

In this group, grown and photographed by Stirling Macoboy, the dome is fitted over a wide, shallow pot.

The driftwood has been used here to give height, and also to support the croton that is growing in the bowl together with the coleus and the moss and small plants at the base.

These domes, placed, as this one is, over a pot of growing plants, provide wonderfully warm and humid conditions that are ideal for tropical plants such as this croton, as well as enhancing their decorative quality. Such plants will grow on for very long periods under these conditions, protected, as they are, from dust and the drying effects of centrally heated rooms.

Very little water is needed, sufficient being provided by the humidity produced, and it is simply a matter of varying the plants from time to time, or supplementing them with one or two cut flowers. These last a long time under glass domes, too.

If the glass becomes misted, it can be raised a little at one side to admit some air. It is a simple matter to remove the dome and give the plants some sun when they become a little drawn from too long indoors.

Flowering Bonsai

The range of flowering trees and plants that can be grown as Bonsai is enormous, and nothing could be more fascinating than achieving a miniature flowering prunus, wisteria, quince, camellia, azalea, or chrysanthemum, to name only a few.

None of these plants is difficult to grow, provided you are enthusiastic enough to devote a little time and patience to them—not a great deal more time, actually, than if they were growing in the open garden; the main difference is that plants growing in shallow containers, as do most Bonsai, require careful and regular watering. Incidentally, the word "Bonsai" originally meant "growing in a shallow vessel," but it has come to be used for all plants grown by a particular method, whatever the shape of their containers. Many beautiful examples of Bonsai are grown in deep and tall pots. The term may also cover low-growing plants and even small bulbs, which one finds included in Japanese books on Bonsai, along with the more traditional treelike forms. Certainly the latter are in the majority, since

A ten-year-old Bonsai *Wisteria sinensis*. One must be prepared for disappointments when growing wisteria in this way. Sometimes they inexplicably fail to flower, or take quite a time to begin flowering. Nevertheless, I believe them to be worth the struggle because of the incredible beauty of a flowering plant when it does decide to rise to the occasion. The flowering period is short, but a little longer than that of vines in the open ground, because potted plants can be lifted to shelter while those outdoors are at the mercy of rain and wind. After flowering, the roots and long growths are pruned, and the plant is given new soil and left in a sunny position. Always give plenty of water.

the tree in miniature is the goal of most growers. There is a trend of late, however, toward a type of miniature garden, complete with a small pool or stream and several plants growing on or in the crevices of stones of various sizes.

These gardens, or rock settings, are not quite the same as the miniature Japanese gardens popular twenty or thirty years ago, which usually bristled with a great assortment of little figures, pagodas, animals, and the inevitable red curved bridge. Western enthusiasts bought these components in Chinese shops and massed them with great exuberance but little regard for plant material in proportion, which probably accounted for the decline of their popularity. The more restrained and authentic Japanese version now coming into favor requires considerable skill, especially in the rock plantings that form an important part of their composition. Although evergreen plants such as pines and junipers are often used, miniature azaleas give a very pleasant note of color and can be adapted quite well to rock planting. Rough weather-worn rocks are the most suitable, and they often have sufficient hollowed-out places to hold the roots of these little plants. A rather heavy soil, containing a little clay to help the roots cling to the rocks, is used; this is then covered with moss, held in place, if necessary, with a little wire until it, too, clings to the rock of its own accord.

The small Gumpo azaleas are well suited to this treatment, and even better is the tiny myrtle-leafed azalea, but a search will reveal a number of possibilities. Bonsai nurseries are now selling plants for this type of arrangement.

Apart from growing the plants on or in the rocks, there are many ways of making these small landscape gardens, some of which are described under the heading, "The Useful Moribana Container." There are now many

Camellia sasanqua Exquisite grown as a Bonsai. Sasanquas have very short-lived flowers when cut, but potted plants will give a good succession of flowers after several years. This one is about eight years old.

70

varieties of these shallow rectangular and oval containers to be found. Some even have a section raised inside to hold a small stream; or one can make a little pool by using one of the hollowed-out stones sometimes found on the mountains or by the seashore. A collection of stones of all shapes and sizes can be used in many ways; moss- or lichen-covered stones are especially beautiful. One can also keep a few stones in the vicinity of, or even in, those trays of moss I have already described, encouraging the moss to grow over them, thus providing a ready-made setting into which small plants or cut branches can be placed as they come to hand.

To grow flowering Bonsai, a sunny place must be found, for unlike the moss gardens, most of these plants need full sun to flower well. Azaleas and Japonica camellias are an exception. A collection can be started from cuttings or seeds, or if quicker results are needed a search of the nurseries will surely reveal any number of possibilities. Do not be dismayed if the plants you like best are in large, ugly cans. If they are a good shape and have a strong-looking treelike trunk, they can easily be cut down to size gradually. This is best done in very late winter or early spring, just when the growing season is about to commence. The plant is taken from its can or pot, most of the old soil is shaken or hosed out, and then the roots are "combed" out so they can be shortened. About one-third is then cut away; if you eventually want to reduce it still further, do so in the second year. The plant is then potted in the shallow Bonsai container. The drainage hole is usually covered with either a square of coarse wire mesh or

Top. This beautiful Bonsai bougainvillaea was grown and trained by Mrs Harold Erdman of Honolulu, Hawaii. The climate there is ideally suited to these heat-loving plants, but they can be grown successfully in semi-tropical and even in relatively cool climates, depending upon the variety. For good results ample sun is essential.

Bottom. This azalea, Empress of India, has been trained to a semi-cascade, and will be encouraged, when new growth starts, to grow farther downwards.

   This variety flowers a little later than the other Indicas, although not so late as the Macranthas, and is a very old, well-known favorite. It is a fairly fast grower, but is easily kept small by pruning its roots each year.

72

an inverted crock, then a thin layer of pebbles or gravel goes over this. My Japanese Bonsai teacher insisted that another layer of smaller gravel and then another layer still smaller should be used, but I never seem to have room for these and the plant, so it really depends on the depth of the container and the size of the plant. If the plant seems to need support a length of wire can be passed through the two drainage holes usually found in these bowls and the two ends twisted together over the roots to anchor them down. Use copper wire for this. Have some special Bonsai soil ready and be sure that it is quite dry so that it can be shaken down into all the crevices between the roots. The soil can be worked in with a sharpened skewer; the Japanese use a chopstick, and if you have one, so much the better. Tap the bowl gently several times to shake the soil well down, and then water it well, or even stand it in a shallow tray of water until the dry soil becomes thoroughly moist. It is very important that, either after the potting operation or before, the top of the plant should be pruned to compensate for the loss of the roots. I prefer to prune after potting, in order to see the shape in relation to the container. The plant will probably require pruning in any case, even if it means the sacrifice of some potential buds, for shape is of the greatest importance. The form will be governed somewhat by the existing shape of the plant, though very great changes can be made if desired, and it is at this stage that any necessary wiring is done. Although most Bonsai are wired at some stage of their lives, this is not always essential for plants that already

These Bonsai chrysanthemums were photographed by Arthur Davis in the courtyard of the lovely Heian Shrine in Kyoto, Japan. One often stumbles across exhibitions of either Bonsai or Ikebana in the famous temples in this fascinating city. Examples such as these are often shown at the all-chrysanthemum shows held during early November in the districts outside Kyoto, and I would urge those who plan to visit Japan in the autumn to make enquiries about these at their hotel or tourist bureau.

The smaller-flowering varieties of chrysanthemum are always used for Bonsai, and a good deal of feeding is needed to produce the abundance of flowers. Nitrogenous fertilizers, or any that produce too much leaf growth, would have to be avoided. Plants must be grown in full sun to keep them sturdy and to promote flower buds.

74

have a graceful shape, such as some azaleas. Azaleas, in fact, are very brittle and hard to wire unless you are quite experienced. A safer method of shaping them is to weigh branches with small pieces of lead to hold them down, or small wires can be tied from the branches to the sides of the pots. This method can sometimes be used in the case of the small crab apples and prunus, but when plants have more flexible branches by all means wind them with a spiral of copper wire, its thickness depending on the size of the branches. Start from the base of the plant and wind carefully upward. The wired branches can then be bent into the shape desired. Do this gently; they can still snap off if you try to hurry the process, and it is better to bend them just a little at intervals of several days.

After you have wired the plant, it should be kept in shade for a week or two to enable it to recover from its repotting before being given gradually more and more sun according to the requirements of its species. Although I excepted azaleas from the full-sun category, some of the smaller types and the Kurumes will take quite a lot of sun and will give more compact masses of flowers under these conditions. The Indica varieties prefer broken shade, as do most of the Japonica camellias. All the fruiting trees and the flowering quince (*Chaenomeles*) like full sun.

Fertilizing is usually best done after flowering, and one can use either one of the soluble fertilizers or, for the fruiting trees, liquid poultry manure. Do not give the latter to the azaleas or camellias, however; it is too alkaline.

This tiny crab apple is about four years old, and was grafted onto dwarf stock to keep it small. This grafting is not always essential, since reasonably small trees can be achieved by buying small nursery plants and keeping their roots and branches pruned each year. This is done in late winter or early spring.

All crab apples need a sunny position, although they can be kept indoors whilst in bloom. When flower petals have fallen, however, they should be again given a sunny place out of doors so that the decorative little apples can be formed. When these are ripe, the plant can again be brought inside and it will look most attractive for quite a few weeks whilst the fruit lasts. The trees may be wired if a special shape is desired, since the branches are quite strong and firm.

Another pruning can be done after flowering, for this is the best time to eliminate surplus twigs and branches. The new growth may then be trained in the way it is to grow.

In the case of fast-growing species, repotting may need to be done once a year. This is the case with wisteria, which has very strong roots. When the plant is turned out of its pot it will soon be apparent if it is running out of soil. Azaleas do not have very big roots, and they and camellias seldom need repotting more often than every two or three years.

I bought this *Wisteria multijuga* (or *floribunda*) *alba* over six years ago, when it was a two-year-old plant in a six-inch pot. I planted it in the ground, intending it to grow against the wall, but so rapid and strong was its growth that I became nervous about the possibility of lifted paving and cracked walls. I therefore dug it up after two years, cut the long top growths and the roots hard back, and put it into a pot just a little larger than the one in which it is shown here. Its period in the ground produced the strong trunk that made wiring unnecessary. During the plant's first four years in the pot no flowers appeared, although there was plenty of growth; but this year the wait has been rewarded, and here it is, flowering just in time for inclusion in this book. It *was* worth waiting for, don't you agree?

Orchids for Glamour

One's view of orchids is inevitably dictated by the climate in which one lives. In the colder parts of America, and in England, for instance, they are still regarded with something like awe; yet I know a lady in Bangkok who keeps her house filled with plastic tulips and daffodils because orchids are so common that everyone has them! In subtropical climates cymbidiums grow in every suburban garden, and many varieties of cattleya can be grown in a cold greenhouse, but even in colder climates the many types of plastic and fiberglass now available, together with cheaper heating methods, mean that a small hothouse can often be acquired without great cost—it can even be added to a balcony or set into a window of an apartment.

Certainly the lovely cattleyas are worth the cost of growing, even though the flowers are not long-lasting. For easier culture and a great length of flowering time, the cypripediums or slipper orchids are well worth considering. Again, your climate will dictate whether or not they can be grown out-of-doors. Rapid air transport is now bringing these orchids to florists all over the world, and the purchase of a plant to keep indoors for the six weeks or more that it blooms can surely be justified, even if the plant must be discarded afterwards.

Here slipper orchids have been submerged, pot and all, among the moss, with some stones to hide the top of the pot. The African violets remain permanently in this bowl. Added height has been given by a branch of deciduous magnolia.

We show here some of the ways that these charming flowers can be used to vary the usual "pot on a windowsill," and, as you see, they can be combined most effectively with other subjects. A little thought and possibly a study of flower-arrangement suggestions will show the many variations that can be played upon the theme of one potted slipper orchid, cattleya, or dendrobium.

The slipper orchids illustrated (*Cypripedium insigne* var. *Sanderae*) grow in a shaded part of our garden underneath a big camellia tree. They are potted in a light porous mixture of coarse leaf mould, sand, and tanbark, and need to be kept damp at all times. Only when they are really climbing out of their pots do we repot them, since they flower best when crowded together. They appreciate a monthly application of liquid soluble fertilizer, especially after flowering, when the new growths are forming.

Top. The slipper orchid is long-lasting and will remain in bloom from four to six weeks if kept in a well-ventilated room. Those shown here have been lifted from their pots and planted in the bamboo trough, where they will remain until their flowers are spent. They will then go back to the pots with some fresh compost, to remain in a sheltered part of the garden in the shade of a tree.

Bottom. Driftwood has been painted with turquoise paint overlaid with silver to serve as a holder for many different types of flowers. Here it complements the lemon and white shades of the slipper orchids.

There is a pleasant harmony of green and gold here between the slipper orchids, the grapes and the Murano ducks. The orchids have been knocked gently out of their earthenware pot and their roots encased in a shallow polythene bag. I have purposely allowed the top of this bag to show in the picture to explain this. It is easily concealed beneath a few small bunches of grapes. This treatment in no way harms the hardy orchids, and they can be left in the bag for several days, provided their roots are kept just moist.

Camellia Arrangements

Camellias are ideal for growing in pots, partly because their small root system allows them to be kept in relatively small containers for long periods, and also because their glossy green leaves remain attractive the whole year round. The flowers are very popular for both classical Western-style and Japanese arrangements, and since many of the latter are designed to create the impression of a growing plant there seems no good reason why an actually growing plant should not be used. Certainly the flowers on such a plant will last longer than cut ones, and when they do fall it is a simple matter to replace them with pinned-on flowers of other, and later, varieties. If sprayed, these will last two or three days, depending upon the variety and room temperature.

Camellia plants lend themselves extremely well to shaping, especially if the smaller, slower-growing types are selected. This is important, remembering that many varieties grow into quite large trees, and, though even these can be dwarfed, it is easier to work with plants less inclined to

Sasanqua camellias adapt well to training as Bonsai, as most of them have a graceful, soft growth habit. They are also very quick and robust growers and therefore need root-pruning each year just after flowering. The one shown here, Exquisite, is about four years old, and when the flowers fade it will be shortened back at the same time as the roots are pruned. Sasanquas will take more sun than the Japonica camellias and, in fact, need sun to promote good blooming, especially when grown in pots.

86

fight restriction. The upright form of the larger camellias cannot be trained into such graceful shapes as the more spreading, softer-branched varieties. Many Bonsai growers use Sasanqua camellias, for these are particularly adaptable, but the Japanese grow a great many of the larger-flowered Higo types as Bonsai.

The relatively strong stems of camellias enable them to be wired to a variety of shapes, but for the more pendulous types wiring is seldom necessary. The single White Czar shown here has not been wired, being merely a healthy small plant growing in a four-inch pot. The branches twine quite easily around pieces of driftwood, and the pot can be concealed behind the base of the wood with the aid of another small curved piece of wood or bark, or the plant can be gently tapped out of its pot and encased in a small plastic or foil bag for a week or so.

Plants growing in decorative glazed pots can be sufficiently ornamental in themselves, especially if they are either grown in the traditional treelike Bonsai form or trained in the "Heaven-earth-man" form of Ikebana. The many variations of this triangular form can be emulated by growing plants, with the great advantage that the growing plants will strengthen and improve as the years go by. Even when not in flower they will be attractive and decorative. They can be kept in a garden or on a balcony or terrace throughout the year, and the training process is easily maintained by nipping off unwanted growths and adding either wires or weights where

Top. Camellia White Czar grows in a small pot concealed behind the green-painted driftwood. When the flowers fall, they can be replaced with cut flowers of the same variety pinned to the same places, or picked with long stems that can be pushed into the soil. Many single white camellias are inclined to drop their heads, even before the flowers are spent, and it is a good idea to drive a fine pin through the calyx as soon as the bloom opens.

Bottom. A small plant of White Tulip camellia growing in a Japanese container, with a few sprays of pussywillow inserted to give added height.

88

necessary. During this growing period try to give the conditions of sun or semi-shade that the particular variety requires. This is as important with camellias as with azaleas or any other potted plants, for camellias vary considerably in their tolerance of sun and shade. Study the catalogues of camellia specialists to find out the requirements of your plants. You will find that the Sasanquas, for instance, like quite a lot of sun — in fact, it is necessary for good flowering — but many of the Japonicas like almost complete shade. The white and red Japonicas usually will take a reasonable amount of sun, while most of the pinks like shade. Broken shade is usually good for most of the Japonicas, but experience with one's own particular aspects and conditions will soon show which each prefers. If leaves become brown and burned-looking it is usually an indication of too much sun. Camellias are not exacting in their requirements. They prefer an acid soil, with a mulch of old cow manure applied after flowering. Liquid fertilizer can be given occasionally, but not after the buds have formed. Remember the rule that fertilizer quantities should be halved for plants growing in pots. It is usually possible to buy prepared camellia soil in bags, and, for the small amount needed for potted plants, this is really the easiest method, especially since these preparations are usually sterilized and well balanced. Mixtures sold for azaleas are also suitable, as are the the special azalea and camellia fertilizers.

The white *Camellia fimbriata* shown here is an old and well-established favorite, and one of the best of the formal whites. It is not a particularly fast grower, and is therefore well suited to growing in containers. As it prefers shade, it can remain indoors while the flowers are in bloom, and they will last better than if exposed to the elements in the garden. The room must be well-ventilated, however, and the soil in the pot kept reasonably damp at all times. This room, in the home of Mr and Mrs Fred Roberts, has a complete wall of glass, so that plants receive ample light.

The smaller camellia is a Sasanqua variety, trained as a Bonsai.

In growing camellias, especially in pots, watering must not be neglected. While old plants growing in the ground will take a certain amount of neglect in this regard, the potted ones must be carefully watched to see that they do not dry out, especially those growing in the shallow Bonsai pots. These will need daily watering in hot weather, and although they can be kept a little drier in winter, remember that this is their flowering time, and the blooms will need a certain amount of water. When the plants are kept indoors, room temperatures will be a governing factor, and central heating will mean more frequent watering. In this, too, experience will be the best guide.

I like to place arrangements of single camellias beneath this painting by Chow Leung Chen-Ying, for the pleasant harmony it creates in the forms of the flowers. The camellias are growing in a four-inch pot concealed behind the green-painted driftwood.

Fuchsias

No amount of skill in the arrangement of flowers can induce the fragile fuchsias to last so long or to look so decorative as they do when grown in standard forms. In this case the variety is Enchanted, a very long-flowering and fairly hardy type that responds quite well to training in this form, though, as the picture shows, the stem needs a good deal of support in its first year. Later it will become stronger, but this one suffered from having its stem almost severed in a high wind. I bound it up with adhesive tape, using a thin twig for a splint, and it grew on apparently unperturbed. The tape is still visible and will be left on for a time. For standards, select single-stem plants of a variety that has strong upright growth; remove all side shoots, but not the leaves growing on the main stem. Pot on as it grows up, so that by the time it has reached the required height there is enough soil to nourish the bushy head; this head forms quickly once the top of the plant is nipped out. Side shoots should be allowed to grow about four inches from the top. As soon as these side shoots have formed two pairs of leaves nip them again, so that more shoots will form. The two shoots that emerge from the cut top are treated in the same way. So it goes on until a round bushy head is formed. Continue the nipping process after the flowers are spent, so that constant new growth is maintained, thus prolonging the flowering season. When this is really over remove all spindly growth and cut back the plant to the harder wood.

Fuchsia Pink Flamingo trained as a Bonsai.

Fuchsias need a rich soil, since they are heavy feeders. For fuchsias in containers a mixture of one part each of sand and peat moss to two parts of good garden loam, with the addition of some well-rotted cow manure, is a good basic diet. Flowers will be improved by applications of weak liquid fertilizer every two to three weeks during the growing season. Again, remember that quantity directions on the packets of all fertilizers to be given to plants in open ground should be halved for those in pots. The rule of "little and often" for fertilizing is a good one for fuchsias.

It is important, too, when training a standard fuchsia, to tie the main stem firmly to the stake every few inches to keep it straight and give it ample support. It is not always necessary, as in the case of the plant illustrated here, to use two stakes. This was done because of the injured stem. After the first season's flowering the plant may need to be potted into a larger container, since the roots are fast-growing. This is best done in spring, when growth is about to begin and while the top is pruned ready for the new shoots. Care will be needed in tapping out the plant from the old pot, to ensure that the stem does not snap. Get a second person to stand by to lift the pot away after its edge has been gently tapped on some projecting ledge to loosen the root-ball, and have the new pot close at hand ready crocked and with some new soil at the bottom. If this is done whilst the plant is dry some of the old soil will fall away, and if any more can be shaken out gently more space for the new soil will be left. Water well, and keep the plant reasonably moist; fuchsias do not like dry conditions. Be sure to keep all fuchsias, not only standards, in as sheltered a position as possible. They like broken shade and complete protection from wind.

The standard fuchsia at the top (Enchanted) is only two years old; that below is only one year old and shows the early stages of training a standard. Fuchsias grow very quickly into standard forms, and can be consolidated in the second year of growth, when the stem will have hardened and become stronger. For tall standards, staking will be necessary with most varieties.

It is not an easy matter to grow fuchsias in Bonsai form. The brittle stems cannot be successfully wired, and in any case the plants grow too quickly for this type of treatment. The best one can do is to look for a plant with a promising shape, eliminate surplus growths, and encourage shoots that form on the remaining branches. These are kept shortened well back to promote flowering.

Some varieties of fuchsias grow very well indoors, others drop their flowers almost at once. Usually the older types make excellent house plants. One must experiment with different varieties and find those best suited to one's own enviroment. In Victorian and Edwardian days these lovely plants were a feature of the conservatories and drawing-rooms, but their adaptability for indoor use seems to have been overlooked in modern interiors.

It is not possible to say just how often to water fuchsias kept indoors; this must also depend on the atmosphere of the room, the season, and whether or not central heating or air-conditioning is used. Never let the soil dry out. One of the reasons why fuchsias grow well in painted or glazed pots is that these retain moisture better than the clay or earthenware pots, so do not be afraid to paint your ordinary pots. You can choose colors that harmonize better with the fuchsias than does the usual red of unpainted pots. Plastic pots are quite satisfactory, too.

Pruning is very important, whether for a special shape or merely to keep plants tidy and floriferous. The rapid growth makes frequent nipping of shoots necessary to prevent the plants from becoming leggy and unattractive.

Eva Borg fuchsia growing in a flat-bottomed wire basket that can be either hung or placed on a stand as shown here. This makes a colorful decoration for an entrance hall or sun-room.

The Invisible Pot

In using potted plants as part of an arrangement, the main problem is hiding the pots. The use today of plastic instead of heavy earthenware pots has made this a simpler matter than it used to be. But, in any case, moving plants from one container to another is a very simple matter, and fears of disturbing a plant that has been bought in flower are usually groundless.

Top. This spathiphyllum is growing in a five-inch pot placed inside the vase, the rim of the pot coming about one inch below that of the vase, so that it gives the impression of an arrangement of cut flowers. The flowers will last for many weeks on the plant if given a shaded position, but one with ample light and air. In warm or subtropical climates spathiphyllum can be grown in a sheltered position in the open, but in colder climates they need to be grown in a greenhouse. They flower best when crowded into their pots, but need rich soil. A good mixture is equal parts of leaf mould, peat moss, and good garden soil, with the addition of some charcoal. They need abundant water.

Bottom. Billbergias grow well in the crowded space of this tall pottery container. They are members of the large family of bromeliads to which the pineapples also belong. Most of them prefer shady positions, which makes them well suited to growing indoors. They are also very hardy, requiring little nourishment, and *Billbergia nutans* grows best if its roots are kept on the dry side. It needs a good light, but not strong sun.

The plant shown here is quite crowded in its pot, and produces more flowers under these conditions. The flowers of the billbergia are short-lived, but wonderful. Do not expect these beautiful flowers to be with you for very long, but grow them in an attractive container so that they can be enjoyed in the house while they last.

Holding the pot in one hand, and covering its surface with the other, while holding the plant between the first and second fingers, tap the edge of the inverted pot on some projecting ledge or shelf. The plant should slip out easily onto the hand, and the new pot should be placed over this inverted plant so that when is it stood upright there will have been no disturbance.

If the plant is being transferred to a larger sized and deeper pot, additional drainage and soil may need to be added first, so that it will not be possible to invert the new pot over the plant, which must be carefully lowered into its new container. This is best done when the plant is on the dry side, for moist soil is apt to fall away more easily.

Sometimes, to make an arrangement, I have taken plants out of pots, left them in the moss gardens or at the base of other plants for several weeks, and then returned them to their original pots. The roots will still be in a compact ball; and even if all the original soil may not still be adhering to them, this is not a cause for alarm: it is a good opportunity to give them new soil and add a little manure to this before repotting.

If unpotted plants are to serve as part of a temporary table arrangement, I often encase the roots in a little nest of either foil or clear polythene. I have made special small bags, just large enough to hold African violet roots, by simply running around the edges of the polythene with the sewing machine; or making a little double pleat at either side may make an even better shaped container. No holes are needed if the arrangement is only to last for several days; but do not give too much water at this time.

The wonderful colors of the recent hybrid polyanthus make them ideal for early spring decoration. Obtainable from many nurseries and stores growing in small plastic pots, they can be either transferred to larger pots, or grouped together in a deep bowl, as they are here.

These are hungry plants, and need weekly applications of liquid fertilizer when grown in small pots. Do not put them in full sun for long periods. They will flower in a well-lighted airy room for two to three weeks if kept well watered and fed.

Left. Here we see again the ever-useful glass dome, this time covering a pot in which grows a Fairy Rose, *Campanula muralis,* and some small ground-covering moss-like plants. Growth under these glass domes is very rapid, as a result of the considerable humidity provided, but air should be admitted fairly freely so that the plants do not become drawn and leggy. Good light is important, too. Just how much light and air will depend on the conditions of the room in which the arrangement is placed, and of course on the season. A little experimenting will soon provide the answers, and a great deal of pleasure can be had from trying out various plant combinations.

Right. Lilium speciosum is very well suited to container culture, and if pots are brought either indoors or to a sheltered position just before the buds open the flowers can be enjoyed at close quarters for several weeks.

A great advantage in growing these beautiful plants in this way is that the pots can be hidden in an out-of-the-way part of the garden during the rather long shabby period of yellowing leaves whilst the bulbs are dying back after flowering.

Cultivation is simple, the main requirement being good drainage. A gritty, open soil mixture is therefore essential, and should consist of one-third coarse sand, one-third leaf mould and one-third rich loam. Most growers place a deep layer of coarse gravelly sand at the bottom of the pot, surrounding the bulbs with sand, then covering to a depth of six to eight inches. Give a general fertilizer several times during the growing season.

Left. A group of African violets in quite small pots have been placed together in this deep Satsuma bowl, where they make a very colorful table centrepiece or a decoration for a hall or side table. The bowl catches the surplus water, and can be moved nearer the light when necessary.

Right. African violets in a brandy glass, arranged and photographed by Stirling Macoboy. The humid atmosphere provided by the curving sides of the glass suits the African violets to perfection, especially if a place near a window with not too much sun is chosen. One must be careful not to pour water into the centre of the plants, lest the buds become too moist and begin to rot. Overwatering must also be avoided because of the lack of a drainage hole.

Tuberous Begonias

In mountain districts, and in climates such as that of England and the cooler regions of the United States, begonias are really at home, and I always remember my envious first sight of them in my father-in-law's English garden, growing right out in the open.

Given such conditions, culture is simple. The begonias can be raised either from seed or from tubers. If you have room for only a few plants it is best to buy them from a nursery or florist when the buds are just beginning to open, for although this is the most expensive way it enables you to choose the colors you want. If you have a greenhouse the seed can be sown in midwinter in finely sieved soil over a deep layer of crocks and kept in a temperature between 60°F. and 70°F. The pots should be covered with a sheet of glass and a sheet of paper. The soil is kept moist by dipping the pots into shallow tepid water. When seedlings appear, gradually give them more light and air each day, and, when they are large enough, pot them in a mixture of one part of leaf mould, one part of sand and three parts of good loam, with a generous sprinkling of dry manure and a sprinkling of bonemeal. As they grow the plants need progressively larger pots. To keep plants sturdy, it is advisable to pick off early flower buds, hard though this is to do.

These beautiful tuberous begonias were photographed in the Conservatory of the Botanic Gardens, Launceston, Tasmania.

Hawaiian Hibiscus

Hawaiian hibiscus are deservedly popular in countries where summers are warm to hot and winters not too chilly.

The plant shown here is only a two-year-old cutting now growing in an eight-inch pot, where, with generous feeding, it will last for the remainder of the summer. By next spring it will require a pot at least another two inches in diameter. I shall leave it in the warmest possible position in the old pot until all danger of frost is over and the days are fairly warm. Then, taking care to disturb the roots as little as possible, I shall transfer it carefully to a larger pot, which will be well crocked and have the richest possible soil in its bottom layer. Only then will the rather shabby-looking old growth be shortened back. There is always a strong temptation to prune hibiscus during winter, when some of the plants look half dead, but it must be resisted until spring. This shabby winter look is one reason why I prefer to grow hibiscus for as long as possible in pots, so that they can be moved out of sight during their dormant period, though they need a warm place at all times. Watering should be reduced in cold weather, and the plants should not be fed.

When the weather is warmer and pruning and repotting are completed, a liberal topping of old animal manure can be given, followed about two months later by an application of artificial general fertilizer. Remember that the amount suggested on the packet should be reduced to almost half for plants growing in pots.

All but very small plants can be pruned quite heavily. For those growing in pots, it is best to cut to a leaf bud or node pointing inward, to make for compactness, since some of the Hawaiian varieties have a rather sprawling habit. When the new shoots have grown to about four inches, nip off the tips; this can be done again when the tips are about two or three inches long. In this way the plants can be made bushier and stronger.

Hibiscus Surfrider, an award-winner in America.

Gloxinias

As with cyclamen and tuberous begonias, gloxinias can be raised from seed or from tubers, or can be bought already in flower from florist or nursery. One great advantage of gloxinias is that one bought plant can be increased to a dozen or more in one season, by propagating from whole leaves or leaf sections. Some type of greenhouse or glass frame would be necessary. Given this, all one has to do is to insert a leaf, preferably with a half-inch or so of stem, into a tray of shell-grit, or sand or peat moss, and to keep it moist for a few weeks. Soon roots will form, and later a small tuber, which will flower beautifully during the next season. The potting mixture can be either a prepared mixture, as is used for African violets, to which they are related, or a mixture made up of one part each of sand, peat moss, old well-rotted cow manure, and leaf mould, with a sprinkling of bonemeal. Weekly applications of weak liquid manure or fertilizer will greatly help flowering, and it is often possible to have a second flowering if, after the first flush is over, the entire stem is cut away and feeding continued. This old stem, with its larger leaves cut away and only the smallest left, can be made into another plant by embedding it in the shell-grit or peat moss tray. What more could one ask of any plant?

If the weather is becoming hot, and the main plant obviously spent, do not try to force it further, but let it dry off gradually and, when all growth has dried up, turn the pots on their sides in a cool part of the greenhouse or lath-house, and leave them to rest until the next year, when shoots will appear to signal time to repot in fresh soil. Tubers will last several years, increasing in size and flowering each year.

A collection of gloxinias.

Achimenes

The dainty achimenes is a small relative of the spectacular gloxinia, having a similar velvety texture in both leaves and flowers, but there the resemblance ends, for these little plants have a soft trailing habit, making them very suitable for growing in hanging baskets. They can, however, be induced to assume a more compact form by the simple process of pinching back the shoots when they are about $1\frac{1}{2}$ or 2 inches high, and again pinching these shoots when they have grown to this length. They should be given as warm a position as possible during this growing period, although the pots can be brought indoors or to a well-lighted porch or balcony when the flowers are ready to open. Water freely during flowering.

After flowering allow the plants to dry off slowly, and the little tubers can either be planted in the ground (in temperate climates) or (in colder regions) stored in a protected dry place.

There is no need to worry unduly about losing track of the quite small tubers in the ground: they can easily be lifted to pots after the shoots appear. Try to retain as much as possible of the soil adhering to the roots in such a case. I grow them around the edges of some large tubs containing citrus trees, where they flourish and multiply in the fertilizer given these trees at intervals during the year. When they have become too numerous, it is easy to lift them from around the edges of the tubs at almost any early stage of growth, and transfer them to decorative pots, as has been done in the case of those illustrated here.

I pot them in one part rich loam, one part leaf mould, and one-half part sand. A fortnightly spraying with a soluble fertilizer will help to prolong flowering.

Achimenes arrangements.

The Banksia Rose has been a favorite for generations. It has been largely eclipsed by newer varieties, but is still seen occasionally, usually growing strongly on walls or archways. Although it is by nature a robust grower, it submits gracefully to the crowded conditions of this glazed Chinese container. When grown in this way, it must be regularly watered and fertilized with any good rose food. After flowering, remove it from the pot, lightly prune its roots and branches, and give it fresh soil. Then place outdoors in a position where it will have plenty of sun. If growth becomes very strong, it may be desirable to repot in a larger container during late winter or early spring.

Azalea and polyanthus with stones. The tall-growing Ruth Marion azalea shown here has been teamed with a group of contrasting polyanthus in a large Moribana type container. The stone is introduced to balance the two groups and to provide solidity. The container was first filled with peat moss enriched by leaf mould, and the polyanthus bedded into this after being knocked out of the very small-sized pots in which they were purchased already in flower. This group will last for quite a time in flower if given the semi-shaded conditions both types of plants prefer. They will receive an application of soluble fertilizer sprayed on to the leaves and flowers and into the soil at intervals of every ten days or so, and this will keep them in good condition for several weeks, depending on the atmosphere in which they are kept. As they are early spring bloomers, they will appreciate being placed out of doors at night rather than being kept permanently in rooms which may still be heated. Remember also that both azaleas and polyanthus like a moist soil, so do not allow them to dry out at any time. Overhead spraying of the flowers will be beneficial, and the appearance of both will be enhanced and the flowering prolonged if all spent flowers are pulled off promptly.

Cherry blossom with growing primroses and helxine. The branch of cherry blossom used here is the single-flowering Japanese cherry which draws thousands of tourists to Japan every April. These lovely blossoms are very delicate and can be very short-lived if subjected to heavy rain or wind, but are well worth growing despite their brief period of glory.

The cut branch was impaled on a needle holder set into a two-inch-deep round tin of water. This is bedded into the peat moss in the container, and it is hidden by the helxine which was lifted from a garden path and laid on the surface. The primroses were bought in small plastic pots and knocked out to also be bedded among the peat moss, but plants of this type could be lifted from the open garden and transferred to such arrangements. Primroses are very easily adapted to this type of treatment, and will continue to grow and flower quite well, for their strong closely packed roots are not easily disturbed. They must, however, be given a rich soil if kept in containers for long periods, and will also require applications of soluble fertilizer at ten-day intervals.

The branch of cherry blossom can be replaced with one of another variety of the many flowering trees that are to be found in early spring, possibly one of the flowering plums or peaches.

Index